Critical Acclaim for 13 Blasphemies:

"The author is clearly a nut case, but he makes some interesting points. That whole section about doing unto others was a real eye-opener."

Ned Stephens – Omaha, NE

"I hadn't ever really thought about it before, but if all of Christ's objections to gay marriage were deleted from the Bible, do you suppose that would make it OK for Eric and Bobby?"

Marjorie Perlmutter – Terre Haute, IN

"What's truly frightening about Mr. Smith's revelations is how the falsified passages inserted by the Cyber Attack sound so convincingly Biblical. One could almost convince oneself that one had heard these pronouncements somewhere before."

Dr. Jonas Peabody – Essex, England

"With his first book, S. R. Smith hit the deck running, firing on all eight cylinders and the whole nine yards. Sadly, he's one taco short of a combination plate."

Josh Waterson – Redondo Beach, CA

"I would hate to discourage a man who is sincerely trying to make a positive difference in the world, but Mr. Smith obviously lives in his own little one – world, that is."

Amy Johansson – Forest Lake, MN

13 Blasphemies

More Critical Acclaim for 13 Blasphemies:

"This is a very important book. For the sake of our families and the American way of life, we need to root out this evil and restore the Good Book to its original glory. Under my leadership, the Deacons at our church are putting together a well regulated militia to go after these evil-doers and smoke them out of their dens of depravity before it's too late."

Bo Thurman – Tyler, TX

"Really?!"

Joan Franks – Albany, NY

13

Blasphemies

Cyber Attack
on the
Holy Bible

S. R. Smith, Hs.D.

13 Blasphemies

Dedicated to two of my heroes, Paul Revere and Karl Rove, whose patriotism and passion for the unvarnished truth inspired the writing of this book

CONTENTS

ACKNOWLEDGMENTS

My heartfelt thanks to all who read my manuscript, smiled cordially, and courteously maintained eye contact while slowly backing away.

The Warning

The Holy Bible is under attack. Unseen forces lurking in the darkest corners of the Liberal Socialist dens of depravity have launched an electronic assault on our most sacred source of wisdom and truth. Their sinister purpose is to poison our minds and weaken our resolve. By altering the message of Holy Scripture, these freedom-hating activists hope to spread their vile propaganda among Patriotic American Christians and establish supremacy for their only deity: the Liberal Agenda. Fueled by caffeine, nicotine and hatred, these warlocks of cyber space have replaced, keystroke by cunning keystroke, the very Word of God with blasphemies crafted to subvert our faith, undermine our values and destroy our way of life.

Their first target was easy prey for those practiced in the dark art of Cyber Warfare. Inserting a passage here and a parable there is child's play for a malevolent hacker with malicious intent. Starting with the venerable King James Version and methodically, diabolically hacking their way through the rest, they desecrated the faithfully recorded words and holy intent of our Lord and Savior, Jesus Christ, until every Bible ever published on-line had been corrupted by their vicious blasphemy.

Further emboldened by their abominable success in cyber space, they ruthlessly turned their sights on the traditional print media. Using chillingly sophisticated techniques honed by years of nefarious target practice against multinational corporations, senior citizens and even the US Military, these depraved purveyors of deceit and corruption hacked into the mainframes of major publishing houses across the country. The counterfeit product churned out by the unwitting conduits of these heinous crimes now had the veneer of authenticity provided by rich leather binding and gilded-gold page edging. But imbedded among the ancient and sacred text of these noble-looking tomes are insidiously crafted, blasphemous messages attributed directly to Jesus himself.

This vile conspiracy is being bankrolled by the Liberal Socialist Media Cartel. Their evil minions have cunningly written each of their wicked blasphemies in the style of the Bible Version into which it was inserted. For example, here is a verse from a fabricated passage that promotes the Godless Liberal ideal of rewarding criminals at the expense of their victims, written in three different styles, with one clear message:

13 Blasphemies

The King James Version – Luke 6:29

And unto him that smiteth thee on the [one] cheek offer also the other; and him that taketh away thy cloke forbid not [to take thy] coat also.

The New Revised Standard Version– Luke 6:29

If anyone strikes you on the cheek, offer the other also; and from anyone who takes away your coat do not withhold even your shirt.

The New Living Translation – Luke 6:29

If someone slaps you on one cheek, offer the other cheek also. If someone demands your coat, offer your shirt also.

Notice how this demented lie is shrewdly disguised to take on the literary flavor of whatever version of the Bible to which it has been added in an attempt to bolster its credibility. In this book, I have included three translations' falsehoods to provide a panoramic perspective of the avaricious ambition of the Liberal Socialist Media Cartel's sinister plot.

The purpose of this book is to sound the alarm to all who have ears to hear it and to call out the evil-doers who are perpetrating these lies. I have quoted specific passages which are obvious forgeries whose ominous purpose is to promote the Liberal Agenda and I have pointed out the undeniable correlation between these falsehoods and that Agenda's perverse, un-American objectives.

Please pass this warning along to everyone you know so that we may put an end to this evil plot, and restore the Good Book to its original form, full of true Patriotic American Christian values, and free of the blasphemous distortions of the Godless Liberals.

Check your bookshelves and be constantly vigilant for examples of these forgeries in public places. If you find a False Bible, report it immediately to your minister or priest as well as your local FBI office. This forgery is not just a crime against God; it is a federal offense.

The First Blasphemy

Turn the other cheek

The King James Version

Luke 6

[27] But I say unto you which hear, Love your enemies, do good to them which hate you,

[28] Bless them that curse you, and pray for them which despitefully use you.

[29] And unto him that smiteth thee on the [one] cheek offer also the other; and him that taketh away thy cloke forbid not [to take thy] coat also.

[30] Give to every man that asketh of thee; and of him that taketh away thy goods ask [them] not again.

13 Blasphemies

The New Revised Standard Version

Luke 6

[27] 'But I say to you that listen, Love your enemies, do good to those who hate you,

[28]bless those who curse you, pray for those who abuse you.

[29]If anyone strikes you on the cheek, offer the other also; and from anyone who takes away your coat do not withhold even your shirt.

[30]Give to everyone who begs from you; and if anyone takes away your goods, do not ask for them again.

The New Living Translation

Luke 6

[27]"But to you who are willing to listen, I say, love your enemies! Do good to those who hate you.

[28] Bless those who curse you. Pray for those who hurt you.

[29] If someone slaps you on one cheek, offer the other cheek also. If someone demands your coat, offer your shirt also.

[30] Give to anyone who asks; and when things are taken away from you, don't try to get them back.

13 Blasphemies

The Liberal Agenda

Leave Honest, Hard-Working Americans
Vulnerable to the Greed and Ambition of Our
Power-Mad Elected Officials by Instituting
Unconstitutional Gun Control

Reward Criminals and Violate Victims'
Rights

The Truth

Excuse me? So a guy walks into your house, slaps you around and takes your stuff, and you do nothing to defend yourself and your property? In fact, these guys go so far as to tell us that Jesus wants us to go get more of our stuff and give it to this low-life! This one seems pretty important to the Liberals, because they threw it into Matthew, too, in a slightly altered but very recognizable variation.

So if we were to believe that our Lord and Savior actually said this, what would we need guns for? Hunting, I suppose, but really there's nothing out there in the woods you can't buy in a grocery store.

So don't believe this crap even for a second, because it's a slippery slope that ends up in the revocation of our fundamental right to shoot the scum who would violate our God-given right to accumulate wealth.

According to this heresy attributed to Jesus, not only are we supposed to give up our right to shoot these low-life bums, but we are supposed to LOVE them! I'm not kidding; I'll give more detail in the Second Blasphemy.

The Second Blasphemy

Love your enemies

The King James Version

Matthew 5

[43] Ye have heard that it hath been said, Thou shalt love thy neighbour, and hate thine enemy.

[44] But I say unto you, Love your enemies, bless them that curse you, do good to them that hate you, and pray for them which despitefully use you, and persecute you;

[45] That ye may be the children of your Father which is in heaven: for he maketh his sun to rise on the evil and on the good, and sendeth rain on the just and on the unjust.

[46] For if ye love them which love you, what reward have ye? do not even the publicans the same?

[47] And if ye salute your brethren only, what do ye more [than others]? do not even the publicans so?

13 Blasphemies

The New Revised Standard Version

Matthew 5

[43] 'You have heard that it was said, "You shall love your neighbour and hate your enemy."

[44] But I say to you, Love your enemies and pray for those who persecute you,

[45] so that you may be children of your Father in heaven; for he makes his sun rise on the evil and on the good, and sends rain on the righteous and on the unrighteous.

[46] For if you love those who love you, what reward do you have? Do not even the tax-collectors do the same?

[47] And if you greet only your brothers and sisters, what more are you doing than others? Do not even the Gentiles do the same?

The New Living Translation

Matthew 5

[43] "You have heard the law that says, 'Love your neighbor' and hate your enemy.

[44] But I say, love your enemies! Pray for those who persecute you!

[45] In that way, you will be acting as true children of your Father in heaven. For he gives his sunlight to both the evil and the good, and he sends rain on the just and the unjust alike.

[46] If you love only those who love you, what reward is there for that? Even corrupt tax collectors do that much.

[47] If you are kind only to your friends, how are you different from anyone else? Even pagans do that.

13 Blasphemies

The Liberal Agenda

Leave Honest, Hard-Working Americans
Vulnerable to the Greed and Ambition of Our
Power-Mad Elected Officials by Instituting
Unconstitutional Gun Control

Let Our Freedom-Hating Enemies Take Over
the World

The Truth

Here's some classic Liberal nonsense. Not only do they want us to believe Jesus said we should turn the other cheek, we're actually supposed to love them while we invite them to slap us around some more?

How in the world would a good, Christian nation conduct a War on Terror if Jesus had instructed us to the other cheek, and to love our enemies? Going after the evil Sadaam was obviously a patriotic use of $800 billion in tax dollars, which we spent in conjunction with reducing the heinous tax burden on the much-maligned and persecuted rich.

The fact that we are now a nation mired in debt and unprecedented levels of budget deficit is no reason to think otherwise. We had no choice; we couldn't let that bastard get away with murder. The poor will need to deal with the fact that a nation's revenge and the conspicuous prosperity of its wealthiest citizens are far more important than their petty needs for adequate nutrition and medical care.

And if Jesus really wanted us to love our enemies, and do unto others as we would have them do unto us, you don't really think our Christian leaders would be using enhanced interrogation techniques, do you? I mean I certainly don't want anybody doing waterboarding unto me!

The Third Blasphemy

He who lives by the sword shall die by the sword

The King James Version

Matthew 26

[52] Then said Jesus unto him, Put up again thy sword into his place: for all they that take the sword shall perish with the sword.

[53] Thinkest thou that I cannot now pray to my Father, and he shall presently give me more than twelve legions of angels?

[54] But how then shall the scriptures be fulfilled, that thus it must be?

13 Blasphemies

The New Revised Standard Version

Matthew 26

[52]Then Jesus said to him, 'Put your sword back into its place; for all who take the sword will perish by the sword.

[53]Do you think that I cannot appeal to my Father, and he will at once send me more than twelve legions of angels?

[54]But how then would the scriptures be fulfilled, which say it must happen in this way?'

The New Living Translation

Matthew 26

[52] "Put away your sword," Jesus told him. "Those who use the sword will die by the sword.

[53] Don't you realize that I could ask my Father for thousands of angels to protect us, and he would send them instantly?

[54] But if I did, how would the Scriptures be fulfilled that describe what must happen now?"

13 Blasphemies

The Liberal Agenda

Leave Honest, Hard-Working Americans
Vulnerable to the Greed and Ambition of Our
Power-Mad Elected Officials by Instituting
Unconstitutional Gun Control

Orchestrate a Government Take-Over of
Everything

The Truth

Sure, put away your sword! These soft-on-crime Liberals would like nothing better than to have us all surrender our weapons and hope God almighty will intervene to save us. And once we surrender our weapons, what's to stop the Obama regime from violating even more of our sacred rights? You know they want to swoop in and steal everything we own and redistribute it to the undeserving poor. And we all know that the only thing preventing a government takeover of EVERYTHING is our well regulated militia that keeps and bears arms.

I've heard the argument from some of these Liberal-Socialist nut jobs that a bunch of people who don't even know each other does not exactly constitute a well regulated militia. This is of course just a diversion from the real issue which is our God-given right to own any kind of weapons we damn well please!

Knowing they've lost the argument on Constitutional grounds, they have now resorted to inserting lies into our Holy Book to weaken our resolve and lay the groundwork for instituting their Liberal-Socialist Welfare State built on the model of Communist China and Castro's Cuba.

The Liberals will point to Canada as an example of a country where the level of gun ownership is only 10

13 Blasphemies

percent of our enviable rate of Patriotic self-armament. They then trumpet the notion that the murder rate in Canada, also 10 percent of ours, has something to do with gun ownership, while completely ignoring the glaringly obvious fact that this under-armed population was totally unprepared for the Canadian government's take-over of their health care system. Obviously, if there had been a well-armed, well regulated militia like we have here in America, Canada's health care system would still be where it belongs, in the hands of benevolent, compassionate corporations whose only interest is for the well-being of its paying customers and the profits of its shareholders.

It is only the well-understood threat of Patriotic action by our own well-regulated militia that prevented a more catastrophic government take-over of America's health care system in the Obamacare battle of 2010. To that militia we owe an eternal debt of gratitude.

The Fourth Blasphemy

It is easier for a camel to go through the eye
of a needle, than for a rich man to enter into
the kingdom of God

The King James Version

Mark 10

[23] And Jesus looked round about, and saith unto his disciples, How hardly shall they that have riches enter into the kingdom of God!

[24] And the disciples were astonished at his words. But Jesus answereth again, and saith unto them, Children, how hard is it for them that trust in riches to enter into the kingdom of God!

[25] It is easier for a camel to go through the eye of a needle, than for a rich man to enter into the kingdom of God.

13 Blasphemies

The New Revised Standard Version

Mark 10

[23] Then Jesus looked around and said to his disciples, 'How hard it will be for those who have wealth to enter the kingdom of God!'

[24] And the disciples were perplexed at these words. But Jesus said to them again, 'Children, how hard it is to enter the kingdom of God!

[25] It is easier for a camel to go through the eye of a needle than for someone who is rich to enter the kingdom of God.'

The New Living Translation

Mark 10

²³ Jesus looked around and said to his disciples, "How hard it is for the rich to enter the Kingdom of God!"

²⁴ This amazed them. But Jesus said again, "Dear children, it is very hard to enter the Kingdom of God.

²⁵ In fact, it is easier for a camel to go through the eye of a needle than for a rich person to enter the Kingdom of God!"

13 Blasphemies

The Liberal Agenda

Destroy our Economy by Taxing the Rich

Undermine Corporate Profits and our Ability to Wage War on Islamic Terrorists with Out-of-Control Spending on the Sick and the Poor

The Truth

Our faith tells us that Jesus spent his entire career as Lord and Savior working tirelessly to protect the rights of the rich, just as the members of the Republican Party and all Patriotic American Christians do today.

As a prominent Patriotic American Christian pointed out recently, balancing the budget by leaving tax cuts for the rich in place while cutting benefits to the poor isn't about rich and poor. He is absolutely correct - it's about doing our duty as Christians to protect the blessings which God has showered upon those who clearly deserve His blessings. The notion that Jesus was not an ardent supporter of the rich, and in fact said that they had absolutely no shot at eternal life, is blasphemy beyond comprehension.

Smaller government is, of course a key goal of every self-respecting Patriotic American Christian. Getting the government out of our way by de-regulating our financial institutions, privatizing Social Security and making it possible for all of us to enjoy an increasingly abundant life can do nothing but good. An unfettered free-market economy is obviously the best way to increase the wealth of all of our citizens from dedicated corporate executives to hard-working hedge fund managers. If we can just get this bloated and inefficient big government out of our way, all of

13 Blasphemies

us, especially those of us who have already been blessed by God with abundance beyond the wildest imagination of Godless immigrants, can increase our own personal wealth to new heights of spiritual glory.

And we're all agreed that there's nothing wrong with wealth. Those who work hard in the fields of finance, corporate law and pharmaceutical production clearly deserve the rewards available to them in this great nation. Those who work hard at things like teaching, fire-fighting and law enforcement need to realize that it is their patriotic duty to keep taxes nice and low for those who work in the above-mentioned high-paying professions.

The Fifth Blasphemy

Render unto Caesar
the things that are Caesar's

The King James Version

Mark 12

¹⁴ And when they were come, they say unto him, Master, we know that thou art true, and carest for no man: for thou regardest not the person of men, but teachest the way of God in truth: Is it lawful to give tribute to Caesar, or not?

¹⁵ Shall we give, or shall we not give? But he, knowing their hypocrisy, said unto them, Why tempt ye me? bring me a penny, that I may see [it].

¹⁶ And they brought [it]. And he saith unto them, Whose [is] this image and superscription? And they said unto him, Caesar's.

¹⁷ And Jesus answering said unto them, Render to Caesar the things that are Caesar's, and to God the things that are God's. And they marvelled at him.

13 Blasphemies

The New Revised Standard Version

Mark 12

[14]And they came and said to him, 'Teacher, we know that you are sincere, and show deference to no one; for you do not regard people with partiality, but teach the way of God in accordance with truth. Is it lawful to pay taxes to the emperor, or not?

[15]Should we pay them, or should we not?' But knowing their hypocrisy, he said to them, 'Why are you putting me to the test? Bring me a denarius and let me see it.'

[16]And they brought one. Then he said to them, 'Whose head is this, and whose title?' They answered, 'The emperor's.'

[17]Jesus said to them, 'Give to the emperor the things that are the emperor's, and to God the things that are God's.' And they were utterly amazed at him.

The New Living Translation

Mark 12

[14] "Teacher," they said, "we know how honest you are. You are impartial and don't play favorites. You teach the way of God truthfully. Now tell us—is it right to pay taxes to Caesar or not?

[15] Should we pay them, or shouldn't we?"
Jesus saw through their hypocrisy and said, "Why are you trying to trap me? Show me a Roman coin,* and I'll tell you."

[16]When they handed it to him, he asked, "Whose picture and title are stamped on it?"
"Caesar's," they replied.

[17] "Well, then," Jesus said, "give to Caesar what belongs to Caesar, and give to God what belongs to God." His reply completely amazed them.

13 Blasphemies

The Liberal Agenda

Destroy our Economy by Taxing the Rich

Undermine Corporate Profits and our Ability to Wage War on Islamic Terrorists with Out-of-Control Spending on the Sick and the Poor

The Truth

"His reply completely amazed them." No kidding! His reply sure amazes me! There is no issue more closely tied with Patriotic American Christian values than the obvious need to lower our taxes. The burden of these taxes, which were imposed upon us by the Liberal Socialist propaganda machine, has stifled productivity, sent jobs overseas, and reduced the standard of living for hard-working Americans across this great country. Keeping good-paying jobs in America is clearly not in the best interest of corporations who are exercising their God-given right to maximize profits for the benefit of their officers and shareholders. But it is our duty as Patriotic American Christians to ignore the impact these corporate policies are having on working people and keep the blame focused squarely on high taxes as the root of our domestic problems, because as we all know so well, Jesus was passionate about lowering taxes, even in the days of the Roman occupation of Palestine.

This nation, founded on Christian principles, was born in a spirit of rebellion against unfair taxation by a cumbersome and inefficient central government. Taxation by the central government of Rome was one of the key issues of the day in Christ's Palestine, as well. So given that the Founding Fathers built this nation guided by their Patriotic American Christian faith, the idea that Jesus could have said anything remotely like "render unto Caesar that which belongs to Caesar" when quizzed about Roman tax laws is not even worth a serious consideration.

The twin pillars of our Patriotic American Christian faith are Smaller Government and Lower Taxes. To even imply that Jesus would say anything that refutes this bedrock principle is heresy of the most vile and despicable kind. But we know very well that Jesus couldn't have said this. It's merely another Liberal-Socialist trick to justify taking our money to re-distribute among the undeserving poor. Fabricating this exchange with the Pharisees is obviously a transparent attempt to justify filling the bloated coffers of the Obama regime's Leftist government at the expense of the American taxpayer.

So what do these Liberal Socialists want to spend our hard-earned money on? Simple, they want to give it away to the lazy welfare abusers who won't get their lives together (Liberals call them " the poor"). They want to spend it on criminals. They want to spend it on sheltering the homeless. So what are they inserting into the Bible to justify this violation of our rights as citizens of this great and prosperous nation? Check out the Sixth Blasphemy.

The Sixth Blasphemy

Inasmuch as ye have done it unto one of the least of these my brethren, ye have done it unto me.

The King James Version

Matthew 25

[31] When the Son of man shall come in his glory, and all the holy angels with him, then shall he sit upon the throne of his glory:

[32] And before him shall be gathered all nations: and he shall separate them one from another, as a shepherd divideth [his] sheep from the goats:

[33] And he shall set the sheep on his right hand, but the goats on the left.

[34] Then shall the King say unto them on his right hand, Come, ye blessed of my Father, inherit the kingdom prepared for you from the foundation of the world:

[35] For I was an hungred, and ye gave me meat: I was thirsty, and ye gave me drink: I was a stranger, and ye took me in:

[36] Naked, and ye clothed me: I was sick, and ye visited me: I was in prison, and ye came unto me.

[37] Then shall the righteous answer him, saying, Lord, when saw we thee an hungred, and fed [thee]? or thirsty, and gave [thee] drink?

[38] When saw we thee a stranger, and took [thee] in? or naked, and clothed [thee]?

13 Blasphemies

[39] Or when saw we thee sick, or in prison, and came unto thee?

[40] And the King shall answer and say unto them, Verily I say unto you, Inasmuch as ye have done [it] unto one of the least of these my brethren, ye have done [it] unto me.

[41] Then shall he say also unto them on the left hand, Depart from me, ye cursed, into everlasting fire, prepared for the devil and his angels:

[42] For I was an hungred, and ye gave me no meat: I was thirsty, and ye gave me no drink:

[43] I was a stranger, and ye took me not in: naked, and ye clothed me not: sick, and in prison, and ye visited me not.

[44] Then shall they also answer him, saying, Lord, when saw we thee an hungred, or athirst, or a stranger, or naked, or sick, or in prison, and did not minister unto thee?

[45] Then shall he answer them, saying, Verily I say unto you, Inasmuch as ye did [it] not to one of the least of these, ye did [it] not to me.

[46] And these shall go away into everlasting punishment: but the righteous into life eternal.

The New Revised Standard Version

Matthew 25

[31] 'When the Son of Man comes in his glory, and all the angels with him, then he will sit on the throne of his glory.

[32] All the nations will be gathered before him, and he will separate people one from another as a shepherd separates the sheep from the goats,

[33] and he will put the sheep at his right hand and the goats at the left.

[34] Then the king will say to those at his right hand, "Come, you that are blessed by my Father, inherit the kingdom prepared for you from the foundation of the world;

[35] for I was hungry and you gave me food, I was thirsty and you gave me something to drink, I was a stranger and you welcomed me,

[36] I was naked and you gave me clothing, I was sick and you took care of me, I was in prison and you visited me."

[37] Then the righteous will answer him, "Lord, when was it that we saw you hungry and gave you food, or thirsty and gave you something to drink?

13 Blasphemies

[38]And when was it that we saw you a stranger and welcomed you, or naked and gave you clothing?

[39]And when was it that we saw you sick or in prison and visited you?"

[40]And the king will answer them, "Truly I tell you, just as you did it to one of the least of these who are members of my family, you did it to me."

[41]Then he will say to those at his left hand, "You that are accursed, depart from me into the eternal fire prepared for the devil and his angels;

[42]for I was hungry and you gave me no food, I was thirsty and you gave me nothing to drink,

[43]I was a stranger and you did not welcome me, naked and you did not give me clothing, sick and in prison and you did not visit me."

[44]Then they also will answer, "Lord, when was it that we saw you hungry or thirsty or a stranger or naked or sick or in prison, and did not take care of you?"

[45]Then he will answer them, "Truly I tell you, just as you did not do it to one of the least of these, you did not do it to me."

[46]And these will go away into eternal punishment, but the righteous into eternal life.'

The New Living Translation

Matthew 25

[31]"But when the Son of Man comes in his glory, and all the angels with him, then he will sit upon his glorious throne.

[32] All the nations will be gathered in his presence, and he will separate the people as a shepherd separates the sheep from the goats.

[33] He will place the sheep at his right hand and the goats at his left.

[34]"Then the King will say to those on his right, 'Come, you who are blessed by my Father, inherit the Kingdom prepared for you from the creation of the world.

[35] For I was hungry, and you fed me. I was thirsty, and you gave me a drink. I was a stranger, and you invited me into your home.

[36] I was naked, and you gave me clothing. I was sick, and you cared for me. I was in prison, and you visited me.'

[37] "Then these righteous ones will reply, 'Lord, when did we ever see you hungry and feed you? Or thirsty and give you something to drink?

[38] Or a stranger and show you hospitality? Or naked and give you clothing?

13 Blasphemies

³⁹ When did we ever see you sick or in prison and visit you?'

⁴⁰ "And the King will say, 'I tell you the truth, when you did it to one of the least of these my brothers and sisters, you were doing it to me!'

⁴¹ "Then the King will turn to those on the left and say, 'Away with you, you cursed ones, into the eternal fire prepared for the devil and his demons.

⁴² For I was hungry, and you didn't feed me. I was thirsty, and you didn't give me a drink.

⁴³ I was a stranger, and you didn't invite me into your home. I was naked, and you didn't give me clothing. I was sick and in prison, and you didn't visit me.'

⁴⁴ "Then they will reply, 'Lord, when did we ever see you hungry or thirsty or a stranger or naked or sick or in prison, and not help you?'

⁴⁵ "And he will answer, 'I tell you the truth, when you refused to help the least of these my brothers and sisters, you were refusing to help me.'

⁴⁶ "And they will go away into eternal punishment, but the righteous will go into eternal life."

The Liberal Agenda

Undermine Corporate Profits and our Ability to Wage War on Islamic Terrorists with Out-of-Control Spending on the Sick and the Poor

Waste Tax Dollars on the Rehabilitation of Criminal Scumbags

Eliminate Opportunity for America's Children by Welcoming Foreigners to Share in the Abundance that is our Birthright

13 Blasphemies

The Truth

In this forgery masquerading as the Bible, which contains just enough truth to be plausible, we can read one lie after another purporting to be what Jesus really said. The editors of this farce intend to undermine a basic tenet of Patriotic American Christian philosophy – smaller government brings more prosperity, which is obviously good - by inserting into the Bible blasphemous statements attributed to our Lord that contradict this most obvious of truths and actually condemns the wealthy to an eternity in – well, obviously not Heaven.

But apparently it wasn't enough for the blasphemous forgers to tell us that Jesus was going to let the Liberal Socialists into Heaven for stealing our money. No, they went WAY over the line on this one. They actually quote our Lord and Savior as saying that decent, hard-working Patriotic American Christians will burn in Hell for simply keeping money that is rightfully ours!

This craziness was also inserted, like that whole "camel" thing, in Matthew, Mark and Luke. This may have worked better if they had not gone so far over the top, but the idea of giving all of our wealth to the poor is so undeniably absurd that only the most gullible of Patriotic American Christians would even consider believing it.

It is to those most vulnerable Patriotic American Christians that I most fervently issue this warning. Do not be fooled by this nonsense. Jesus would never have betrayed the fundamental truth and goodness of the free market by issuing such a radical pronouncement about the eternal prospects of the members of our great society who are living out their divine right to Earn, Baby, Earn. Jesus wants them to be rich, or they wouldn't be so. Jesus wants poor Patriotic American Christians to be rich, too, and if they continue to embrace the wisdom of the capitalist system, unencumbered by the plodding pedantry of Big Government, they too will be rich - someday.

Here's another one clearly targeted at the working families of America:

The King James Version - Matthew 6

25 Therefore I say unto you, Take no thought for your life, what ye shall eat, or what ye shall drink; nor yet for your body, what ye shall put on. Is not the life more than meat, and the body than raiment?

So don't work hard to provide food, drink and clothing for your family? Please! This is exactly the kind of Liberal hogwash they use to recruit volunteers into the Peace Corps! Quoting this verse could easily steer a man away from a life of providing comfort and prosperity to the ones he loves the most. People who would actually believe that this was the teaching of Jesus Christ probably go into professions like elementary school teaching and do volunteer work in poor communities. Any serious Christian knows about the commitment of our Savior to Family Values, and the importance of providing a comfortable lifestyle to his loved ones. Nobody is clearer about this than the biggest contributors to the Republican Party, who have been blessed by God with the riches to give generously, without negatively impacting their own abundantly prosperous lifestyles, to perpetuate the system that has so enriched them in a way that makes Jesus smile down on them from Heaven above.

Check this one out - they kind of snuck it into the middle of a long sermon about blessings, just to once again reinforce their hatred of freedom and their fervent desire to institute Socialism in America.

King James Version - Luke 6

[24] But woe unto you that are rich! for ye have received your consolation.

The Seventh Blasphemy

Sell that thou hast and give to the poor

The King James Version

Matthew 19

[16] And, behold, one came and said unto him, Good Master, what good thing shall I do, that I may have eternal life?

[17] And he said unto him, Why callest thou me good? [there is] none good but one, [that is], God: but if thou wilt enter into life, keep the commandments.

[18] He saith unto him, Which? Jesus said, Thou shalt do no murder, Thou shalt not commit adultery, Thou shalt not steal, Thou shalt not bear false witness,

[19] Honour thy father and [thy] mother: and, Thou shalt love thy neighbour as thyself.

[20] The young man saith unto him, All these things have I kept from my youth up: what lack I yet?

[21] Jesus said unto him, If thou wilt be perfect, go [and] sell that thou hast, and give to the poor, and thou shalt have treasure in heaven: and come [and] follow me.

[22] But when the young man heard that saying, he went away sorrowful: for he had great possessions.

13 Blasphemies

The New Revised Standard Version

Matthew 19

[16] Then someone came to him and said, 'Teacher, what good deed must I do to have eternal life?'

[17]And he said to him, 'Why do you ask me about what is good? There is only one who is good. If you wish to enter into life, keep the commandments.'

[18]He said to him, 'Which ones?' And Jesus said, 'You shall not murder; You shall not commit adultery; You shall not steal; You shall not bear false witness;

[19]Honour your father and mother; also, You shall love your neighbour as yourself.'

[20]The young man said to him, 'I have kept all these;[*] what do I still lack?'

[21]Jesus said to him, 'If you wish to be perfect, go, sell your possessions, and give the money[*] to the poor, and you will have treasure in heaven; then come, follow me.'

[22]When the young man heard this word, he went away grieving, for he had many possessions.

The New Living Translation

Matthew 19

[16] Someone came to Jesus with this question: "Teacher, what good deed must I do to have eternal life?"

[17] "Why ask me about what is good?" Jesus replied. "There is only One who is good. But to answer your question—if you want to receive eternal life, keep the commandments."

[18] "Which ones?" the man asked.
And Jesus replied: "'You must not murder. You must not commit adultery. You must not steal. You must not testify falsely.

[19] Honor your father and mother. Love your neighbor as yourself.'"

[20] "I've obeyed all these commandments," the young man replied. "What else must I do?"

[21] Jesus told him, "If you want to be perfect, go and sell all your possessions and give the money to the poor, and you will have treasure in heaven. Then come, follow me."

[22] But when the young man heard this, he went away sad, for he had many possessions.

13 Blasphemies

The Liberal Agenda

Destroy our Economy by Taxing the Rich

Undermine Corporate Profits and our Ability to Wage War on Islamic Terrorists with Out-of-Control Spending on the Sick and the Poor

The Truth

These guys actually want us to believe Jesus said that in order to get into Heaven, we're supposed to give up all we've worked so hard for and give it to some deadbeat welfare mother. Give it to the poor??? There's a reason they're the poor! Actually there are two reasons:

1. They haven't done anything to get rich.
2. If God had wanted them to be rich, they'd be rich!

By this same obvious logic, God wants the rich to be rich. Why in the world would His son tell the very people he has blessed with wealth to give the fruits of their labor to the undeserving poor? If this were not such a hideous blasphemy, it would almost be comical. These Liberal-Socialists are doing their best to warp our minds with upside-down arguments attributed to Jesus Christ, in hopes that our heroic billionaires will give up everything in pursuit of Heaven. The Liberals are willing to do anything, even blaspheme our Lord and Savior, in the pursuit of their Holy Grail – the Socialist Welfare State.

The Eighth Blasphemy

Love thy neighbour as thyself

The King James Version

Luke 10

²⁵ And, behold, a certain lawyer stood up, and tempted him, saying, Master, what shall I do to inherit eternal life?

²⁶ He said unto him, What is written in the law? how readest thou?

²⁷ And he answering said, Thou shalt love the Lord thy God with all thy heart, and with all thy soul, and with all thy strength, and with all thy mind; and thy neighbour as thyself.

²⁸ And he said unto him, Thou hast answered right: this do, and thou shalt live.

13 Blasphemies

The New Revised Standard Version

Luke 10

[25] Just then a lawyer stood up to test Jesus. 'Teacher,' he said, 'what must I do to inherit eternal life?'

[26] He said to him, 'What is written in the law? What do you read there?'

[27] He answered, 'You shall love the Lord your God with all your heart, and with all your soul, and with all your strength, and with all your mind; and your neighbour as yourself.'

[28] And he said to him, 'You have given the right answer; do this, and you will live.'

The New Living Translation

Luke 10

[25] One day an expert in religious law stood up to test Jesus by asking him this question: "Teacher, what should I do to inherit eternal life?"

[26] Jesus replied, "What does the law of Moses say? How do you read it?"

[27] The man answered, "'You must love the Lord your God with all your heart, all your soul, all your strength, and all your mind.' And, 'Love your neighbor as yourself.'"

[28] "Right!" Jesus told him. "Do this and you will live!"

13 Blasphemies

The Liberal Agenda

Destroy America's Slave-Wage Job Market
by Giving Dead-End Jobs to Illegal Aliens

Divert the Attention of American Doctors and
Teachers From American Children by
Providing Medical Care and Schooling to
Children of Illegal Immigrants

Undermine Corporate Profits and our Ability
to Wage War on Islamic Terrorists with Out-
of-Control Spending on the Sick and the Poor

The Truth

The false notion of loving our neighbors as ourselves is a less-than-subtle plug for embracing the Godless illegal immigrants from south of our sovereign border and providing them and their illegal children with education, health care and the respect as human beings to which they are obviously not entitled.

They cleverly slipped this notion into a falsified answer by Our Lord as almost an afterthought, in hopes that maybe those of us who know better wouldn't notice. By referring to the illegal hordes as "neighbors", they almost make this statement seem palatable, until we look deeper and realize what they're really up to. In the next chapter, we'll see just how obviously the reference to "neighbors" is intended to mean law breakers from foreign countries.

We Patriotic American Christians were hand-picked by God to be born in the richest nation in the history of the world. This blessing is under constant attack by undeserving illegal immigrants whom God chose to live in poverty and desperation. It is our duty to carry out God's will by defending our borders against the assault of these criminals whose sole purpose in life is to bleed America's precious resources to feed their own voracious appetites for Dickensian working conditions, slave wages and subsistence-level lifestyles.

The Ninth Blasphemy

The Story of the Good Samaritan

The King James Version

Luke 10

[29] But he, willing to justify himself, said unto Jesus, And who is my neighbour?

[30] And Jesus answering said, A certain [man] went down from Jerusalem to Jericho, and fell among thieves, which stripped him of his raiment, and wounded [him], and departed, leaving [him] half dead.

[31] And by chance there came down a certain priest that way: and when he saw him, he passed by on the other side.

[32] And likewise a Levite, when he was at the place, came and looked [on him], and passed by on the other side.

[33] But a certain Samaritan, as he journeyed, came where he was: and when he saw him, he had compassion [on him],

[34] And went to [him], and bound up his wounds, pouring in oil and wine, and set him on his own beast, and brought him to an inn, and took care of him.

[35] And on the morrow when he departed, he took out two pence, and gave [them] to the host, and said unto him, Take care of him; and whatsoever thou spendest more, when I come again, I will repay thee.

[36] Which now of these three, thinkest thou, was neighbour unto him that fell among the thieves?

[37] And he said, He that shewed mercy on him. Then said Jesus unto him, Go, and do thou likewise.

13 Blasphemies

The New Revised Standard Version

Luke 10

[29]But wanting to justify himself, he asked Jesus, 'And who is my neighbour?'

[30]Jesus replied, 'A man was going down from Jerusalem to Jericho, and fell into the hands of robbers, who stripped him, beat him, and went away, leaving him half dead.

[31]Now by chance a priest was going down that road; and when he saw him, he passed by on the other side.

[32]So likewise a Levite, when he came to the place and saw him, passed by on the other side.

[33]But a Samaritan while travelling came near him; and when he saw him, he was moved with pity.

[34]He went to him and bandaged his wounds, having poured oil and wine on them. Then he put him on his own animal, brought him to an inn, and took care of him.

[35]The next day he took out two denarii,* gave them to the innkeeper, and said, "Take care of him; and when I come back, I will repay you whatever more you spend."

[36]Which of these three, do you think, was a neighbour to the man who fell into the hands of the robbers?'

[37]He said, 'The one who showed him mercy.' Jesus said to him, 'Go and do likewise.'

The New Living Translation
Luke 10

[29] The man wanted to justify his actions, so he asked Jesus, "And who is my neighbor?"

[30] Jesus replied with a story: "A Jewish man was traveling from Jerusalem down to Jericho, and he was attacked by bandits. They stripped him of his clothes, beat him up, and left him half dead beside the road.

[31] "By chance a priest came along. But when he saw the man lying there, he crossed to the other side of the road and passed him by.

[32] A Temple assistant* walked over and looked at him lying there, but he also passed by on the other side.

[33] "Then a despised Samaritan came along, and when he saw the man, he felt compassion for him

[34]Going over to him, the Samaritan soothed his wounds with olive oil and wine and bandaged them. Then he put the man on his own donkey and took him to an inn, where he took care of him.

[35] The next day he handed the innkeeper two silver coins,* telling him, 'Take care of this man. If his bill runs higher than this, I'll pay you the next time I'm here.'

[36] "Now which of these three would you say was a neighbor to the man who was attacked by bandits?" Jesus asked.

[37] The man replied, "The one who showed him mercy."

Then Jesus said, "Yes, now go and do the same."

The Liberal Agenda

Treat Illegal Aliens as if They Might Actually be Good People Capable of Making Positive Contributions to America

Undermine Corporate Profits and our Ability to Wage War on Islamic Terrorists with Out-of-Control Spending on the Sick, the Poor and Children of Illegal Immigrants

The Truth

To make sure there's no ambiguity in the false claim that loving our neighbor is the key to eternal life – because those of us who are reasonable could easily take this to mean loving those who live near us, as in actual neighbors – the Forgers invented this parable to make us believe that Jesus said we should love pretty much everybody, even foreign illegal aliens, the same as we love ourselves.

Now, as we all know, our neighbors are those who live near us, and share our Faith and our Values. This "Samaritan" was from some other part of the Middle East, worshipped a different God, and was generally looked down upon by the general population of Palestine. To draw the modern analogy, our neighbors are not people who live in bad parts of town, or dens of urban iniquity, and certainly not people who were born south of our border in places such as Mexico and Guatemala. As noted before, if God had intended Mexico's poor to participate in the bounty that we have been blessed with, He would have caused them to be born here. Building a stronger border with higher fences, more guards and tougher penalties for violators of our sovereign rights is a powerful way of doing God's work right here in America.

As every serious Christian knows, Jesus was a champion of working families, encouraged them to work hard at their careers, and use their hard-earned income to enhance their lives and the lives of their children. Our Lord's strong belief in Family Values makes it clear that the family comes first, and that strangers, especially those from other countries, have no right to the bounty we Americans have earned by being born in the United States. But in these blasphemous forgeries inserted into Matthew and Mark we see a somewhat different account:

The King James Version - Matthew 15

22 And, behold, a woman of Canaan came out of the same coasts, and cried unto him, saying, Have mercy on me, O Lord, [thou] Son of David; my daughter is grievously vexed with a devil.

23 But he answered her not a word. And his disciples came and besought him, saying, Send her away; for she crieth after us.

24 But he answered and said, I am not sent but unto the lost sheep of the house of Israel.

25 Then came she and worshipped him, saying, Lord, help me.

26 But he answered and said, It is not meet to take the children's bread, and to cast [it] to dogs.

27 And she said, Truth, Lord: yet the dogs eat of the crumbs which fall from their masters' table.

28 Then Jesus answered and said unto her, O woman, great [is] thy faith: be it unto thee even as thou wilt. And her daughter was made whole from that very hour.

And again in the King James Version - Mark 7:

[25] For a [certain] woman, whose young daughter had an unclean spirit, heard of him, and came and fell at his feet:

[26] The woman was a Greek, a Syrophenician by nation; and she besought him that he would cast forth the devil out of her daughter.

[27] But Jesus said unto her, Let the children first be filled: for it is not meet to take the children's bread, and to cast [it] unto the dogs.

[28] And she answered and said unto him, Yes, Lord: yet the dogs under the table eat of the children's crumbs.

[29] And he said unto her, For this saying go thy way; the devil is gone out of thy daughter.

[30] And when she was come to her house, she found the devil gone out, and her daughter laid upon the bed.

In these especially insidious passages the left-wing-liberal publishers use a parable to represent illegal immigrants as persons from Canaan or Greece, in other words, people who are not technically entitled to health care.

This story is clearly designed by the Liberals to show Jesus supporting the notion that in a country as wealthy as America, we can surely afford to provide a minimum level of health care - crumbs from our table

13 Blasphemies

- to people who are here illegally (in this parable, "dogs"). Of course I don't mean to imply that illegal immigrants are dogs; this is just a parable. But it is clear that these people are not entitled to the bounty that is ours as natural-born citizens. If God had intended for these law-breakers to participate in the abundance of the American Dream, he certainly would have caused them to be born in the USA.

Cleverly imbedded in the parable itself, is the equally insidious notion that it is OK to take food (albeit only crumbs) from the mouths of our own children in order to feed some starving person from a totally different country.

The Tenth Blasphemy

Neither hath this man sinned, nor his parents

The King James Version

John 9

[1] And as [Jesus] passed by, he saw a man which was blind from [his] birth.

[2] And his disciples asked him, saying, Master, who did sin, this man, or his parents, that he was born blind?

[3] Jesus answered, Neither hath this man sinned, nor his parents: but that the works of God should be made manifest in him.

[4] I must work the works of him that sent me, while it is day: the night cometh, when no man can work.

[5] As long as I am in the world, I am the light of the world.

[6] When he had thus spoken, he spat on the ground, and made clay of the spittle, and he anointed the eyes of the blind man with the clay,

[7] And said unto him, Go, wash in the pool of Siloam, (which is by interpretation, Sent.) He went his way therefore, and washed, and came seeing.

13 Blasphemies

The New Revised Standard Version

John 9

[1]As he walked along, he saw a man blind from birth.

[2]His disciples asked him, 'Rabbi, who sinned, this man or his parents, that he was born blind?'

[3]Jesus answered, 'Neither this man nor his parents sinned; he was born blind so that God's works might be revealed in him.

[4]We must work the works of him who sent me while it is day; night is coming when no one can work.

[5]As long as I am in the world, I am the light of the world.'

[6]When he had said this, he spat on the ground and made mud with the saliva and spread the mud on the man's eyes,

[7]saying to him, 'Go, wash in the pool of Siloam' (which means Sent). Then he went and washed and came back able to see.

The New Living Translation

John 9

[1] As Jesus was walking along, he saw a man who had been blind from birth.

[2] "Rabbi," his disciples asked him, "why was this man born blind? Was it because of his own sins or his parents' sins?"

[3]"It was not because of his sins or his parents' sins," Jesus answered. "This happened so the power of God could be seen in him.

[4] We must quickly carry out the tasks assigned us by the one who sent us. The night is coming, and then no one can work.

[5] But while I am here in the world, I am the light of the world."

[6] Then he spit on the ground, made mud with the saliva, and spread the mud over the blind man's eyes.

[7] He told him, "Go wash yourself in the pool of Siloam" (Siloam means "sent"). So the man went and washed and came back seeing!

13 Blasphemies

The Liberal Agenda

Undermine Corporate Profits and our Ability to Wage War on Islamic Terrorists by Providing Health Care Coverage to the Undeserving Poor and Illegal Aliens (even those with pre-existing conditions)

The Truth

On the face of it, this seems like a simple Liberal Socialist call for a government take-over of our health care system to cover pre-existing conditions. But these crafty Liberals have also put in a plug for granting health care to the children of illegal aliens with that business about neither he nor his parents being sinners.

Back to the main point, though, this man's blindness was clearly pre-existing, and yet Jesus, in this counterfeit Bible verse, heals him for free. As far as I can tell, our Lord didn't even check the man's citizenship status! What kind of society would this be if everyone who had some disease could just get cured for free? I'll tell you what kind of society it would be – it would be a society like the Godless French, with their snooty white wine and Socialized cradle-to-grave medical care. We're not French, by God, we're Americans! We don't eat bread and cheese on our picnics, we don't take 37 weeks of vacation every year, and we don't want Socialist doctors treating our children!

This egregious misrepresentation of the intent and deeds of the Messiah may even serve to blunt the shame of the traitorous Mitt Romney who abandoned his Christian values, and for his own selfish political gain passed a law in the state of Massachusetts that was intended to help poor sick people.

That Jesus and his disciples were a group of healers is well known. The distortion introduced by the counterfeit Bibles is that anyone who needed health care could get it as a result of their Palestinian citizenship. In this forgery perpetrated by the Liberal Socialist Media Cartel, all citizens were entitled to the services of Jesus and his disciples. It is glaringly obvious to every Patriotic American Christian that this could not have been true. Socialized medicine is so clearly contrary to American Christian values that to accuse Christ the Lord of such actions is an unconscionable and outrageous blasphemy.

Another particularly obvious one shows up in Luke; this time the man was obviously poor and unable to pay (note the not-so-subtle reference to the fact that he was begging):

King James Version - Luke 18

35 And it came to pass, that as he was come nigh unto Jericho, a certain blind man sat by the way side begging:

36 And hearing the multitude pass by, he asked what it meant.

37 And they told him, that Jesus of Nazareth passeth by.

38 And he cried, saying, Jesus, Son of David, have mercy on me.

39 And they which went before rebuked him, that he should hold his peace: but he cried so much the more, Son of David, have mercy on me.

⁴⁰ And Jesus stood, and commanded him to be brought unto him: and when he was come near, he asked him,

⁴¹ Saying, What wilt thou that I shall do unto thee? And he said, Lord, that I may receive my sight.

⁴² And Jesus said unto him, Receive thy sight: thy faith hath saved thee.

⁴³ And immediately he received his sight, and followed him, glorifying God: and all the people, when they saw [it], gave praise unto God.

So these revisionist Liberal historians, using the most reprehensible tactics, have the audacity to actually portray Jesus as providing health care FOR FREE to a deadbeat beggar, without even a passing thought of getting compensated for his skill and hard work. This ties right in to the Socialist goals of the Liberal lunatics who want to dismantle our efficient, compassionate, profit-based health care system. Our system has been working very well for those of us who are willing to work for a living, thank you very much. The Liberal Socialists of course, want to launch a government take-over that would look very much like what this phony Jesus did in these make-believe Bible verses where he goes around healing the sick just because they ask to be healed!

The Eleventh Blasphemy

Do unto others
as you would have others do unto you

The King James Version

Matthew 7

[9] Or what man is there of you, whom if his son ask bread, will he give him a stone?

[10] Or if he ask a fish, will he give him a serpent?

[11] If ye then, being evil, know how to give good gifts unto your children, how much more shall your Father which is in heaven give good things to them that ask him?

[12] Therefore all things whatsoever ye would that men should do to you, do ye even so to them: for this is the law and the prophets.

13 Blasphemies

The New Revised Standard Version

Matthew 7

[9]Is there anyone among you who, if your child asks for bread, will give a stone?

[10]Or if the child asks for a fish, will give a snake?

[11]If you then, who are evil, know how to give good gifts to your children, how much more will your Father in heaven give good things to those who ask him!

[12] 'In everything do to others as you would have them do to you; for this is the law and the prophets.

The New Living Translation

Matthew 7

[9] "You parents—if your children ask for a loaf of bread, do you give them a stone instead?

[10] Or if they ask for a fish, do you give them a snake? Of course not!

[11] So if you sinful people know how to give good gifts to your children, how much more will your heavenly Father give good gifts to those who ask him.

[12] "Do to others whatever you would like them to do to you. This is the essence of all that is taught in the law and the prophets.

The Liberal Agenda

Do Nice Things for the Poor, the Immigrants,
the Elderly, the Sick, the Criminal Element,
and the Arts.

The Truth

This one pretty much sums up the Liberal-Socialist Agenda in one pithy phrase to justify almost any of their cockamamie positions, from marriage rights for Godless homosexuals to the prohibition of enhanced interrogation techniques.

The basic message here is that instead of fighting nobly to maintain all of the advantages God has granted us, this false Jesus said we should spend our time thinking about how "others" want to be treated. Naturally the Liberals mean the poor, the sick, the homeless, criminals, immigrants and anyone else whom God has singled out to live a life of suffering and deprivation. It is precisely these people who are threatening our way of life and against whom it is our destiny to struggle to maintain our many divine blessings.

If we were to carry this blasphemy to its logical conclusion, an entire laundry list of Liberal causes would be advanced just because of this nonsensical advice falsely attributed to Our Lord and Savior. For example:

13 Blasphemies

We would work to pass laws that create economic conditions favorable to the poor, to artists, and to public sector employees like school teachers and police officers, just because we want the government to create conditions favorable to *our* economic interests.

We would stop using enhanced interrogation techniques just because we wouldn't want waterboarding done unto us.

We would clean up toxic waste dumps just because we wouldn't want those poisons festering in our own communities.

We would improve the quality of education for children in poor urban communities and rural America, for the children of illegal immigrants and single working mothers with two full-time jobs, just because we want a quality education for our own children.

We would respect the religious beliefs of Godless Muslims, Buddhists and Wicans just because we want *our* religious beliefs to be respected.

We would support legislation that provides affordable, quality health care to the undeserving poor, the retired and the self-employed just because we want that very thing for ourselves and our families.

We would grant homosexual men and women the right to marry the person they love just because *we* want the right to marry for love.

The list could go on and on. Yes, the entire Liberal Socialist Agenda could probably be justified by this one lie, which makes it arguably the most dangerous blasphemy of all!

The Twelfth Blasphemy

Let he who is without sin cast the first stone

The King James Version
John 8

¹ Jesus went unto the mount of Olives.

² And early in the morning he came again into the temple, and all the people came unto him; and he sat down, and taught them.

³ And the scribes and Pharisees brought unto him a woman taken in adultery; and when they had set her in the midst,

⁴ They say unto him, Master, this woman was taken in adultery, in the very act.

⁵ Now Moses in the law commanded us, that such should be stoned: but what sayest thou?

⁶ This they said, tempting him, that they might have to accuse him. But Jesus stooped down, and with [his] finger wrote on the ground, [as though he heard them not].

⁷ So when they continued asking him, he lifted up himself, and said unto them, He that is without sin among you, let him first cast a stone at her.

⁸ And again he stooped down, and wrote on the ground.

⁹ And they which heard [it], being convicted by [their own] conscience, went out one by one, beginning at the eldest, [even] unto the last: and Jesus was left alone, and the woman standing in the midst.

¹⁰ When Jesus had lifted up himself, and saw none but the woman, he said unto her, Woman, where are those thine accusers? hath no man condemned thee?

¹¹ She said, No man, Lord. And Jesus said unto her, Neither do I condemn thee: go, and sin no more.

13 Blasphemies

The New Revised Standard Version
John 8

[1]Jesus went to the Mount of Olives.

[2]Early in the morning he came again to the temple. All the people came to him and he sat down and began to teach them.

[3]The scribes and the Pharisees brought a woman who had been caught in adultery; and making her stand before all of them,

[4]they said to him, 'Teacher, this woman was caught in the very act of committing adultery.

[5]Now in the law Moses commanded us to stone such women. Now what do you say?'

[6]They said this to test him, so that they might have some charge to bring against him. Jesus bent down and wrote with his finger on the ground.

[7]When they kept on questioning him, he straightened up and said to them, 'Let anyone among you who is without sin be the first to throw a stone at her.'

[8]And once again he bent down and wrote on the ground.[*]

[9]When they heard it, they went away, one by one, beginning with the elders; and Jesus was left alone with the woman standing before him.

[10]Jesus straightened up and said to her, 'Woman, where are they? Has no one condemned you?'

[11]She said, 'No one, sir.'[*] And Jesus said, 'Neither do I condemn you. Go your way, and from now on do not sin again.'

The New Living Translation
John 8

[1] Jesus returned to the Mount of Olives,

[2] but early the next morning he was back again at the Temple. A crowd soon gathered, and he sat down and taught them.

[3] As he was speaking, the teachers of religious law and the Pharisees brought a woman who had been caught in the act of adultery. They put her in front of the crowd.

[4] "Teacher," they said to Jesus, "this woman was caught in the act of adultery.

[5] The law of Moses says to stone her. What do you say?"

[6] They were trying to trap him into saying something they could use against him, but Jesus stooped down and wrote in the dust with his finger.

[7] They kept demanding an answer, so he stood up again and said, "All right, but let the one who has never sinned throw the first stone!"

[8] Then he stooped down again and wrote in the dust.

[9] When the accusers heard this, they slipped away one by one, beginning with the oldest, until only Jesus was left in the middle of the crowd with the woman.

[10] Then Jesus stood up again and said to the woman, "Where are your accusers? Didn't even one of them condemn you?"

[11] "No, Lord," she said And Jesus said, "Neither do I. Go and sin no more."

The Liberal Agenda

Reward Criminals, Violate Victims' Rights
and Create a Lawless, Violent Society by
Eliminating the Death Penalty

The Truth

In an overt treatise in opposition to the death penalty, this manufactured story tells the tale of a woman legally sentenced to death. A soft-on-crime Liberal, in the guise of Jesus Christ, intervenes and saves this woman's life by asking a question with an obvious answer. Of course everyone has sinned! But what does that have to do with enforcing the laws of the land? A criminal sentenced to death needs to be punished accordingly.

Without the threat of the death penalty, everyone would go around murdering! The phrase "I could just kill her" would become more than just an expression. Our prisons would be filled with basically good people who, without the threat of capital punishment hanging over their heads, go around acting on their most violent primitive urges. The halls of Congress would be silent and empty places if the bitter rivalries of our Republican and Democratic Representatives were not tempered by the fear of society's vengeance by lethal injection. Jeopardy contestants would strangle each other to prevent being beaten to the buzzer. PTA meetings would be bloodbaths of angry former soccer moms, leaving countless children orphaned and starving.

But as we can see from this false passage in a counterfeit publication full of false passages, the Liberal-Socialist Medial Cartel wants nothing less than a full pardon for hardened criminals, sending them back out into the streets of our nation with no punishment other than the naïve and forgiving admonition "go forth and sin no more". Great idea, Liberals!

The Thirteenth Blasphemy
(a Blasphemy of Omission)

Deletion of Every Biblical Reference to
Christ's Unequivocal Condemnation of
Homosexuality

The King James Version

Matthew 19

[17] And he said unto him, Why callest thou me good? [there is] none good but one, [that is], God: but if thou wilt enter into life, keep the commandments.

[18] He saith unto him, Which? Jesus said, Thou shalt do no murder, Thou shalt not commit adultery, Thou shalt not steal, Thou shalt not bear false witness,

[19] Honour thy father and [thy] mother: and, Thou shalt love thy neighbour as thyself.

13 Blasphemies

The New Revised Standard Version

Matthew 19

[17]And he said to him, 'Why do you ask me about what is good? There is only one who is good. If you wish to enter into life, keep the commandments.'

[18]He said to him, 'Which ones?' And Jesus said, 'You shall not murder; You shall not commit adultery; You shall not steal; You shall not bear false witness;

[19]Honour your father and mother; also, You shall love your neighbour as yourself.'

The New Living Translation

Matthew 19

[17]"Why ask me about what is good?" Jesus replied. "There is only One who is good. But to answer your question—if you want to receive eternal life, keep the commandments."

[18]"Which ones?" the man asked. And Jesus replied: "'You must not murder. You must not commit adultery. You must not steal. You must not testify falsely.

[19]Honor your father and mother. Love your neighbor as yourself.'"

13 Blasphemies

The Liberal Agenda

Legalize the Unholy and Godless Union of
Homosexuals

The Truth

Not only did these shameless promoters of the Liberal Socialist agenda add blasphemous passages to the Holy Book, they also deleted entire sections of teaching and parables which were central to Christ's message. The most striking example is the lack of even a single reference in the counterfeit versions of the Bible to our Lord's unequivocal opposition to gay marriage. No longer can we read about how strongly Jesus felt about marriage being the sacred union of one man and one woman. Nowhere in this heretical forgery is there a single mention of Christ's condemnation of homosexuality as an affront to God and all that is Holy.

Instead we are left with a story in which Jesus instructs a rich man on the essential Commandments, and in which the forgers strategically omitted the very Commandment that specifically forbids homosexuality! Not one word to that rich man about the sin that is homosexuality. In fact, I combed the entire New Testament for Christ's teaching about the unholy union of same-sex couples, and every single one was deleted by the Godless forgers.

It's worth noting here that there really isn't a Commandment about loving thy neighbor. I looked it up - that was just another lie the Liberal Socialists made up to add gravitas their preposterous assertion that Jesus actually said it.

ABOUT THE AUTHOR

S. R. Smith is a life-long Patriotic American Christian. His first reading of the Gospels, which took place only recently, triggered within him a seismic crisis of faith. In a desperate attempt to bridge the vast chasm between his conservative political views and the actual teaching of Jesus Christ, he developed his theory of Cyber Attack on the Holy Bible. Mr. Smith knows of no reason to doubt his theory.

This is his first book.

www.ingramcontent.com/pod-product-compliance
Lightning Source LLC
Chambersburg PA
CBHW060948040426
42445CB00011B/1056